Kingskerswell

of Yesteryear

**Chips Barber
& John Hand**

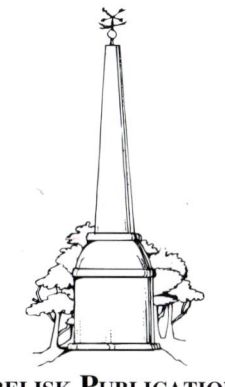

OBELISK PUBLICATIONS

OTHER OBELISK PUBLICATIONS
Around and About the Haldon Hills – Revisited, *Chips Barber*
Pub Walks in and around the Haldon Hills, *Brian Carter*
The Templer Way, *Derek Beavis*
Pictures of Paignton, Parts I, II and III, *Peter Tully*
Torquay, *Chips Barber*
Paignton, *Chips Barber*
Brixham, *Chips Barber*
Newton Abbot Album, Parts I and II, *Fred Tozer*
Newton Abbot in the News, *Brian Thomas*
The Ghosts of Berry Pomeroy Castle, *Deryck Seymour*
The Great Little Totnes Book, *Chips Barber*
The Ghosts of Totnes, *Bob Mann*
Kingsteignton Collection, *Richard Harris*
Kingsteignton of Yesteryear, *Richard Harris*
The Teign Valley of Yesteryear, Parts I and II, *Chips Barber*
Around the Churches of the Teign Valley, *Walter Jacobson*
Brixham of Yesteryear, Parts I, II and III, *Chips Barber*
From Brixham… With Love, *Chips Barber*
The Ghosts of Brixham, *Graham Wyley*
Murders and Mysteries in Devon, *Ann James*
Ten Family Walks on Dartmoor, *Sally and Chips Barber*
Six Short Pub Walks on Dartmoor, *Sally and Chips Barber*
Circular Walks on Eastern Dartmoor, *Liz Jones*
Railways on and around Dartmoor, *Chips Barber*
Devon's Railways of Yesteryear, *Chips Barber*
Around and About Teignmouth, *Chips Barber*
Ghastly and Ghostly Devon, *Sally and Chips Barber*
Weird and Wonderful Dartmoor, *Sally and Chips Barber*
Haunted Pubs in Devon, *Sally and Chips Barber*
Made in Devon, *Chips Barber and David FitzGerald*
Place-names in Devon, *Chips Barber*

We have over 180 Devon-based titles; for a list of current books please send SAE to 2 Church Hill, Pinhoe, Exeter, EX4 9ER or telephone (01392) 468556

*First published in 2002 by
Obelisk Publications, 2 Church Hill, Pinhoe, Exeter, Devon
Designed and Typeset by Sally Barber
Printed in Great Britain
by Colour C Ltd, Tiverton, Devon*

© **Chips Barber & John Hand/Obelisk Publications 2002**

All Rights Reserved. No part of this publication may be reproduced, stored in a retrieval system, or transmitted, in any form or by any means, electronic, mechanical, photocopying, recording or otherwise, without the prior permission of the publishers and copyright holders.

Kingskerswell
of Yesteryear

With thirteen letters, Kingskerswell is one of the longer place-names of Devon. The first part of its name implies royal ownership, whilst the second and third parts name its physical attributes. These would have been deemed important by early settlers, as the presence of springs or wells was a deciding factor in the development of any settlement. But this is no history book; we will be looking at Kingskerswell as portrayed by photographers, thereby limiting ourselves to just a brief period of time.

We are very grateful to Mr Gale, Mr Palmer and Mrs Matthews for the loan of these pictures, which they have collected throughout the years. For some places – like Cockington, Torquay, Brixham or Clovelly – there is an abundance of material, but in non-tourist locations such as Kingskerswell it is rare to find such a wonderful collection.

We begin at the top end of Fore Street looking towards Fluder Hill, where a group of young lads are stood outside the butcher's shop, probably in the early years of the twentieth century. The name French is clearly displayed above the window. Oliver French is listed as the butcher in a 1931 county directory.

Kingskerswell of Yesteryear

On the opposite page (top) is the 'back road' to Newton Abbot, favoured by people who like to avoid traffic queues at Penn Inn roundabout! Whitpot Mill Tea Gardens, shown here in the 1920s, is no more, but many people remember it well. The middle picture shows a 'Comfy Car' taking a group of locals for a day's outing. Below that is Water Lane, as seen from Torquay Road.

On this page we have two views of Kerswell Arch, now just a memory to those who used to pass through it when travelling between Newton Abbot and Torquay. The arch served its purpose for about sixty years before it was dismantled in the early 1960s, to be replaced by a steel and concrete single-span bridge. The lower picture shows the work in hand, with a group of councillors studying the plans.

Kingskerswell of Yesteryear

The two photographs on this page were taken at Broadgate Lodge, which has now been turned into flats and is barely visible from the new road level.

In the beautiful composition below Bessie Luscombe is feeding the chickens, which had the run of the orchard.

An attractive dwelling set in extensive grounds, the house above was Broadgate; now in its place are the houses and gardens of Broadgate Road. This picture postcard was posted from Congresbury, in Somerset, on 24 September 1903.

Below is a later view of the village, about 1938, as seen from the 'Downs', looking across Aller Vale. The church of St Mary lies just a little to the left of centre but is partly obscured by trees. It was taken at a time when the village, mid way between Torquay and Newton Abbot, had seen mushroom growth.

In the age before widespread telephone ownership (and a life-time before e-mail) it was common to send postcards with the briefest of greetings. The card above was sent to distant Torquay by someone in Kingskerswell to wish their sister, Alice, a Happy New Year. The picture shows the view of roof-tops as seen from Tor Hill.

Below we see the thatched Tor Hill Cottage. The postcard was sent, on 28 September 1905, to the same person to thank her for a parcel.

The picture above is looking towards the main village street from the direction of Rose Hill. What is particularly pleasing about pictures of this era, is that they depict street scenes with little or no traffic; it must have been pure bliss to be a cyclist in those days.

If your eyesight is good, you will see a gentleman walking up the road on the left side of the picture below. Just to the right of his head, you may see the letters GWR, these being on a train passing through Kingskerswell's station. The caption on this card has a spelling mistake, but we will let you discover it for yourself.

Having looked up Fore Street, it's now time to look down it in the opposite direction. The postcard shown above was posted by 'Alice' from Yatton in Somerset to Miss B. Howard of Southernhay Farm, Kingskerswell on 6 July 1905.

Although Kingskerswell still has a good number of shops, in the past it had a lot more. In an age when ordinary people didn't have motor cars, local shops were all-important to everyday life – and the village had the full range.

Kingskerswell of Yesteryear

The sight of a photographer setting up a tripod in the street was enough to engender plenty of interest in the youngsters. All four of the pictures shown on these two pages have drawn the attention of spectators.

Above is Trott's Seven Stars Hotel, demolished in the 1960s to make way for building the new bridge on the A380. It seems to be a tradition to have a pub of this name in villages whose church is dedicated to St Mary, as is the case with Kingskerswell.

Below, on the right hand side of a muddy Fore Street, the premises of H. Taylor, oil merchant, can be spied. This later became Sagars Ironmongers, but is now the chemist's shop.

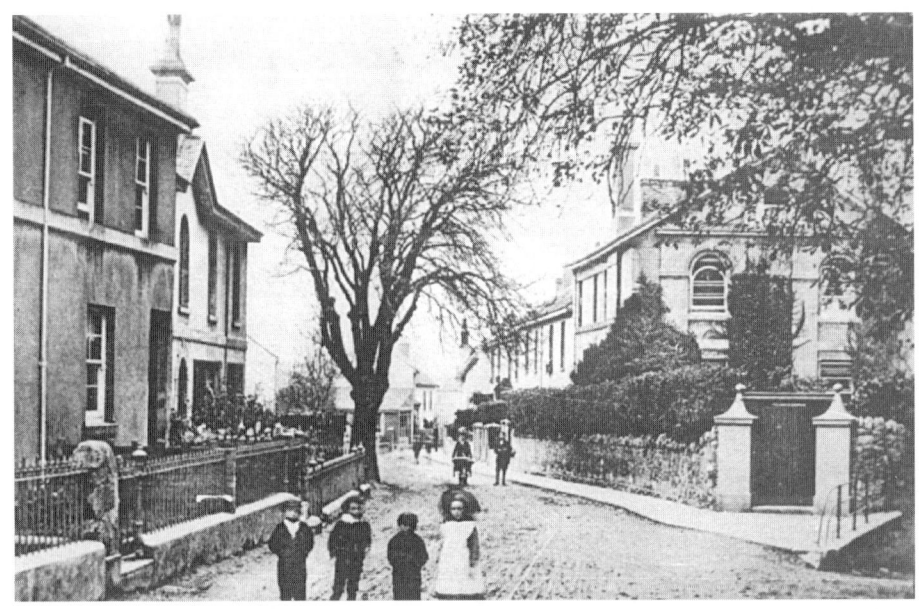

The lack of greenery on the wonderful chestnut tree above is proof that this is a non-summertime photo. It was taken in about 1901, and the lad second from the left has been identified as a member of the Fogwill family.

The postcard below was sent on 13 February 1906.

Kingskerswell of Yesteryear

Above is Kingskerswell's school with a number of pupils gathered in the playground.

Shown below is the cast of *The Magic Key*, a play in three acts, at one of the two perfomances which were staged at the Constitutional Hall just before Christmas 1932.

Here, and across the middle pages, we have pictures of 'Beating of the Bounds' on 6 September 1923. The route was followed precisely and in both these scenes maps are being consulted. For posterity, included in the superb picture spanning pages 16 and 17 are: Evelyn Wonacott, Kathleen Warman, Dorothy Dyer, Miss Opie, Winnie Honeywell, Mrs Gill, Donald Gill, Mrs Taylor (née Dorothy Davey), Miss Heard, Mrs Roberts, Mrs Jury, Mrs Mason (née Eileen Best), Ena Wyatt, Mrs Blackler (née Ruth Coombes), Mrs Davey, Reg Wyatt, Jack Matthews, Mrs Clarke, Percy Bradford, Tom Dart, Donald Honeywell, H. Whiteway, Bill Tozer and Jim Wakeham. We wonder just how many grandparents, and even great-great-grandparents, are shown in this picture? If the 'feat' was repeated today, it's extremely unlikely that anyone would sport ties!

Kingskerswell of Yesteryear

Kingskerswell of Yesteryear

In 1966 the bounds were beaten again, this time on 30 August. The pictures opposite show most of the merry throng who participated that day. Taken at Compton Castle, the top scene shows some of the stalwarts who also featured in the 1923 outing. The pictures below were taken in Coffinswell Lane.

Above is a small crowd of happy drinkers; to our right we have a group of skittlers.

Below are a number of local girls posing by the Maypole. They include Carol Warren, Pat Binmore, Josy Binmore, Beth Webber, Val Gill, Diana Rowe, Jacky Thorne, Geraldine Thorne and Janet Jones.

Kingskerswell of Yesteryear

The picture above is from 1928 and shows: (back row, left to right) Bill Owen, Louis Triggs, Victor Aggett, Frank Gale, Henry Hall, Len Matthews and Harold Dart; (second row) Freda Dart, Sybil Garrett, Joan Searle, Evelyn Wonnacott, Winnie Brown, Grace Dart, Betty Jennings and Peggy Andrews; (third row) Wilfred Richards, Arthur Nicks, Evelyn Knapman, Mary Gully, Clara Butt, Marjorie Mitchell, Marie Mortimer, Albert Williams and Stanley Richards; (front row) ?, Cyril Simpson, Clarence Wilkinson, Roland Elliott, Ronald Channing, Kevin Dogger, Morris Kernick and Ronald Hearne.

Below, the picture is possibly from the summer of 1929 and shows many of the same faces. In addition we have Viola Powling, Becky Mortimer, Ern Wyatt, Cyril Martin, Dennis Murphy, Ken Sampson, Jack Terrell, Mary Cole, Percy Drake, Joyce Germon, Donald Pack, Bessie Stentiford, Ted Stentiford and Iris Brown.

On this page headmaster Mr W. R. Weaver is featured sporting plus-fours! The picture above is from 1932/33 and includes many of the faces shown opposite, with the further addition of Frank Gale, Peggy Osborne, Wilf Howard, Ron Channing, Myrtle Gater, Betty Wallen, Joe Uren, Harold Evans, Cosmo Hill, Norman Howard, Eddie Crocker and Charlie Brooking.

The class shown below lined up, in about 1933, as follows: (back row) Kevin Dogger, Freda Dart, Marie Mortimer, Phyllis Field, Claudine Trout, Eva Gigg, Iris Brown, Mary Cole, Marjorie Babbage and Bob Huggins; (second row) Peter Murphy, Roy Hill, ? Watson, Doris Wonnacott, Thelma Evans, Joyce Smale, Joyce Germon, Evelyn Knapman, Marion Petherick, Kathleen Hatherley, Gwen Nicks, George Moon (?) and David Kernick; (third row) Ted Stentiford, Hubert Wickens, Arnold Symons, Elsie Brooking, Amy Aggett, Rita Snell, Dolly Searle, Margaret Jury, John de Pledge, Roland Elliott and Donald Paul; (front row) John Kench, John Kivell, George Moon (?), ? Watson, George Gater, Jabez Petherick, ? Kivell, Frank Vowden and Ken Sampson.

Kingskerswell of Yesteryear

Opposite (top) is a 1930 view, as seen from a garden in Willake Road.
The sheep in the middle scene are in a field adjacent to Southey Lane, running just above them.
The bottom picture was taken at Jury's Corner, long before The Sloop was built.
Above is a view of Westhill House, taken in about 1900. Just about visible are two people on the right and four on the left, members of the Jury family.
Below is Westhill Terrace, the photo being taken just before the First World War. It shows the main Newton to Torquay road before it was widened. No traffic lights were needed at this junction in those days!

Kingskerswell of Yesteryear

The top two pictures opposite show a bungalow being built in the 1920s, on the Newton road, not far from what is now The Sloop public house. Below them, the view is from the rear of the Public Hall, showing Elmside and Brookhill.

Above, we see Mr Jury with Carlo the dog, outside the front door of Westhill House.

Below is an aerial photo from 1981, showing the same area.

At one time there were a great many potteries, and therefore potters, in the district; above are two workers at the Aller Vale Pottery. Arthur Pearse is on the right.

Below is the bridge spanning what was then part of the Great Western Railway. The telegraph pole, almost in the centre of the view, is the same one which appears to the right of the picture at the top of the opposite page. What looks like a bungalow is revealed as a very tall stationmaster's house and booking office!

Kingskerswell's station was most entertainingly described by Deryck Seymour in his book *The Magic Triangle* (Obelisk Publications, 1993) as follows: *At the end of the viaduct stood a tall three-storeyed building, and to buy a ticket you entered at street level to be greeted by a fast closed door with 'Stationmaster' inscribed thereon. Hurrying past this in case the great man should appear, you descended by a steep staircase to the next floor where was the Booking Office. It was at this point that one always heard the train coming. Hastily grabbing a ticket and dashing down*

another flight of stairs, you emerged breathless onto the up platform, just in time to see the train pull out. To catch a train from the down platform was even worse because, after buying your ticket, you had to climb up to street level again, walk the length of the viaduct and then run down about forty steps to the train. Obviously it was very easy to miss a train at Kingskerswell, and to add to your misery, collected on the bridge, could be a crowd of jeering youngsters enjoying the sight of perspiring grown-ups missing their trains.

Now the up platform boasted a signal box where dwelt a very matey signalman who was always ready to discuss the wonders of his geraniums; but the down platform completely eclipsed its neighbour by boasting a truly remarkable gents' loo. Its shape was most peculiar, its designer having begun with a rectangle but attached to this semicircular ends. It was of solid iron and had formidable spikes all round the top. Was this freak of platform furniture designed by the great Brunel himself in a whimsical moment, or was it a standard piece of equipment?

Kingskerswell of Yesteryear

The picture above dates back to 1906; although the writing on the banner is indecipherable, we know that it said 'Success to the Maypole Dance'. Of the two young girls wearing sashes, the shorter one later became Mrs Pearse, whilst the taller one became Mrs Warman. Below are the members and mascot of Kingskerswell United AFC's team of the 1923/1924 season.

The picture opposite (top) dates back to the mid-1940s. The ones below are from the 1980s, taken at the 'new' primary school in Coffinswell Lane.

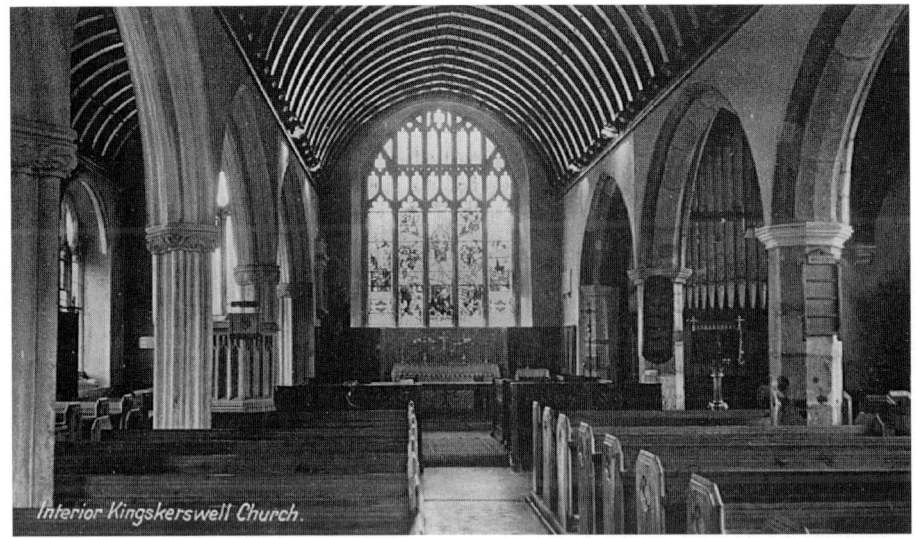

Interior Kingskerswell Church.

Opposite (top) is a group of men outside the Seven Stars in the 1940s. The ladies in the middle picture include Mrs Cornish, Eileen Bishop, Kit Warman, Gwen Wyatt and Mrs Oliver Stentiford. It was taken during the Coronation celebrations of 1953.

In 1938, this was published in Arthur Mee's *Devon*: *Kingskerswell... has the charm of thatched cottages, a brook running by its churchyard, an orchard with the scanty ruins of a castle where the Dinhams lived for centuries, and a church where dwellers at the castle and simple village folk have lain for ages past. Most of the church was made new in the 15th century, but its tower is a century older. There are old stocks in the porch, an ancient font, and among the medieval glass in the east window can be seen a head of St George, a figure of St Jerome, and fragments of St Christopher and St Anthony. The graceful lamps of hammered ironwork were made by local blacksmiths. The Vicarage was built, in 1836, at the instigation of the Rev Aaron Neck.* This building is now offices on Fore Street, whilst the modern vicarage is a bungalow in Pound Lane.

Just look at the state of the road in the picture above, which shows the parish church of St Mary on the left. *The Devon Village Book*, produced by the WI, informed its readers that: *The church, built before Domesday, was probably originally of timber with a thatched roof – a long building to include chancel and nave, but with no aisles. How times have changed!*

(Below) Taken before the First World War, we see a wider view of the village, which has grown enormously in the last century.

We hope that you have enjoyed this photographic trip down the streets of a Kingskerswell of Yesteryear.